CANDY COUNTING

• delicious ways to add and subtract •

841 ooey-gooey words by Lisa McCourt
+36 lip-smackin' pictures by Brad Tuckman
———————
1 really funny book

Troll

BridgeWater Books

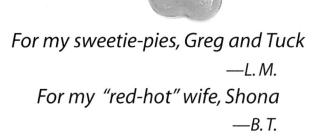

For my sweetie-pies, Greg and Tuck

—L. M.

For my "red-hot" wife, Shona

—B. T.

A special thanks to Dr. Brian E. Enright, National Training Network,
and to Judy Boll and her second grade class.

Text copyright © 1999 by Lisa McCourt.
Illustrations copyright © 1999 by Brad Tuckman.

Published by BridgeWater Books, an imprint and registered trademark of Troll Communications L.L.C.

Book design by Cheryl Nathan.
Produced by Boingo Books, Inc.

Printed in the United States of America.

10 9 8 7 6 5 4 3 2 1

Library of Congress Cataloging-in-Publication Data

McCourt, Lisa.
Candy counting: delicious ways to add and subtract /
841 ooey-gooey words by Lisa McCourt ; + 36 lip-smackin' pictures
by Brad Tuckman [equals] 1 really funny book.
p.   cm.
Statement of responsibility appears as an addition problem on t.p.
Summary: Presents addition and subtraction story problems
involving lollipops, taffy, gumballs, peppermints, fudge and other types of candy.
ISBN 0-8167-6329-1
1. Addition Juvenile literature. 2. Subtraction Juvenile literature.
[1. Addition. 2. Subtraction.] I. Tuckman, Brad, ill. II. Title.
QA115.M385   1999
513.2'11--dc21   99-21929

A child's first experience with math can be intimidating. Or it can be as much fun as counting candies! This book assures a positive introduction to early math concepts by combining funny story problems with mouthwatering candy art that will engage the imagination of any young reader.

Read each story with your child and talk to him or her about how to figure out the problem. Discovering the math problem hidden within the words is the key to success with story problems. Have your child try to answer the question by counting the candies on the page. Then turn to the answers in the back of the book and point out how each story problem represents a math problem. With practice, your child will grasp the connections.

It's easy to continue the game in your home and turn your child into a math detective by looking for the math in daily routines. You'll be laying the best possible foundation for building future math skills. See page 32 for some suggestions!

Taffy, caramels, fudgy treats—this book is good enough to eat! If you like candy and you like counting stuff, get ready for a sweet game. Read each of these tasty questions and see if you can figure out the answer by counting the candies in the picture. Sometimes you'll get the answer by counting all the candies. Sometimes you'll get it by counting the candies in smaller groups. The words will give you the clues you need so you'll know what to do. If you get stuck on one, take a guess. It's just for fun—and all the answers are in the back anyway!

You visit the eye doctor on Monday, the ear doctor on Tuesday, and the belly-button doctor on Wednesday. Each doctor gives you 1 lollipop. How many doctor's-office lollipops will you eat this week?

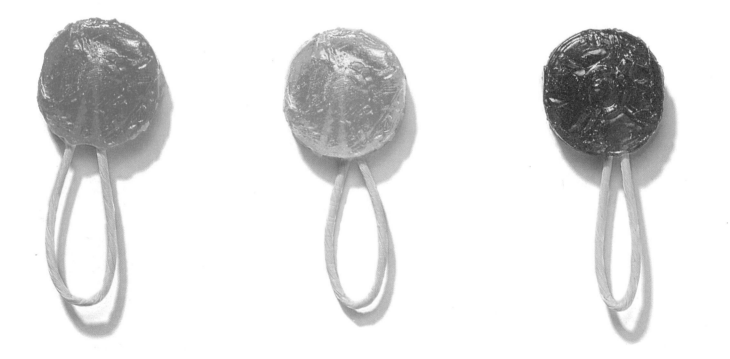

It's Mother's Day! You make your mom a beautiful necklace of gummy rings. You want it to have all her favorite colors. So you use 2 green gummy rings, 2 yellow gummy rings, and 2 red gummy rings. How many gummy rings do you use?

You want to play with your dog, Ruffy. But he's asleep under the kitchen table. You shoot 1 of your gumballs near him. He keeps snoozing. You shoot 8 more gumballs. Ruffy leaps to his paws! He gobbles up all the gumballs you fired at him. How many gumballs does Ruffy eat?

Your grandpa always smells like the butterscotch candies he carries in his pockets. He comes to visit for 7 days. Every day he gives you 1 butterscotch candy. If you save them all up until he leaves, how many butterscotch candies do you have?

You have 4 pieces of taffy. Your best friend also has 4 pieces. But 2 of hers are green. Your best friend hates all green foods! She gives her green pieces to you. How many pieces of taffy do you have now? How many does she have?

Your little brother piles 10 caramels into his toy dump truck. He leaves the truck in the hot summer sun while he watches an ant carry a really big leaf across the driveway. Then he remembers his truck! When he tries to dump the melty caramels, 6 gooey globs are stuck. How many caramels get dumped?

11

Whack! You hit the piñata at your birthday party. It breaks and 30 peppermints fly out! While you are still blindfolded, the kids at your party grab up 30 peppermints. How many are left for you?

You have 18 jawbreakers. It's bowling day in the pretend world of your dolls. Barb B. needs 1 bright blue ball to go with her bowling shoes. Her friend Kent needs 1 red one. Red is his lucky color. How many jawbreakers are left to suck on?

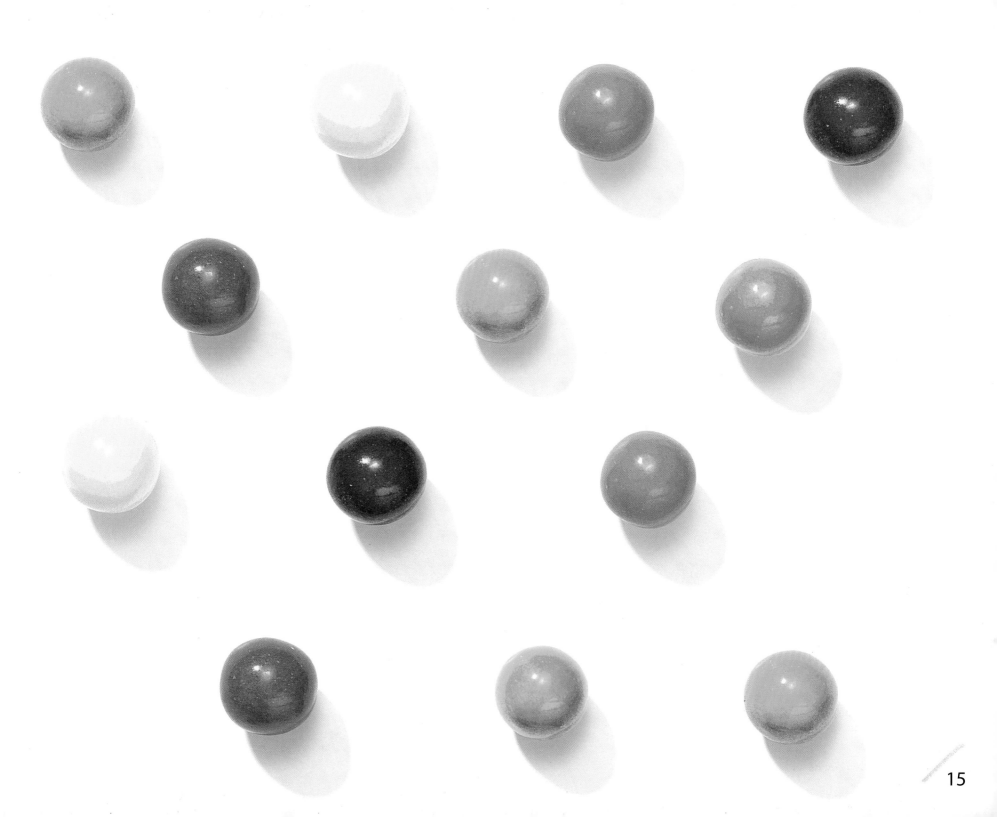

It's Valentine's Day! You want to give candy hearts to 28 friends. You need another 1 for your teacher. And, of course, you need 1 for your best valentine, your mom. In all, how many valentine candy hearts do you need?

At the scouting cookout, you're the first in line to toast marshmallows. You have a long stick, so you ask for 9. But trying to spear all those marshmallows is hard. Suddenly you feel a big sneeze coming. Splat! Splat! Splat! You drop 3 marshmallows into the mud. How many marshmallows do you have left to toast?

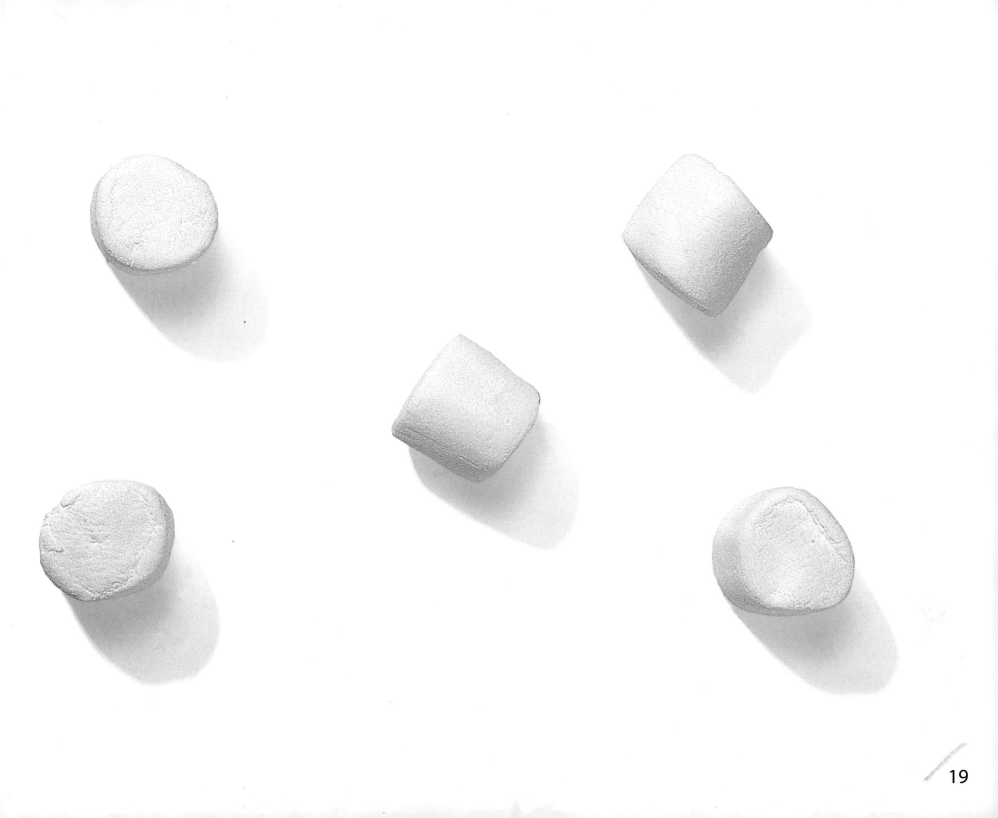

The only good thing about visiting your Aunt Beatrice is her dish of red-hots. You politely take only 6 and put them in your pocket. But when she's not looking, you stuff in 20 more. How many red-hots are in your pocket?

On the way home, 10 red-hots fall out of the hole in your pocket. How many do you have now?

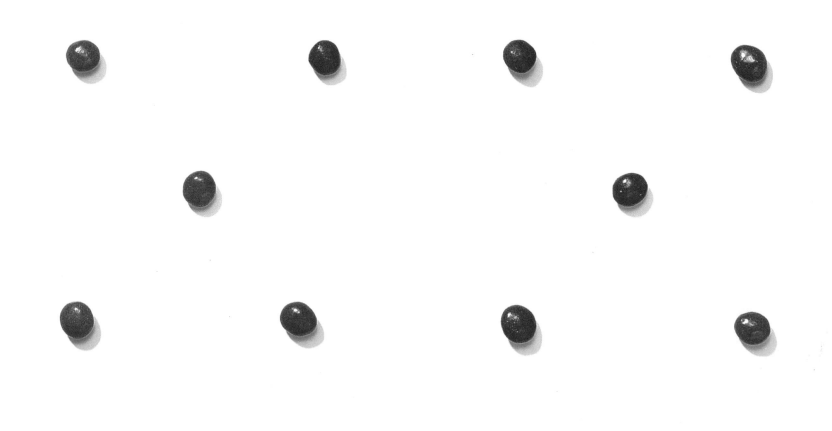

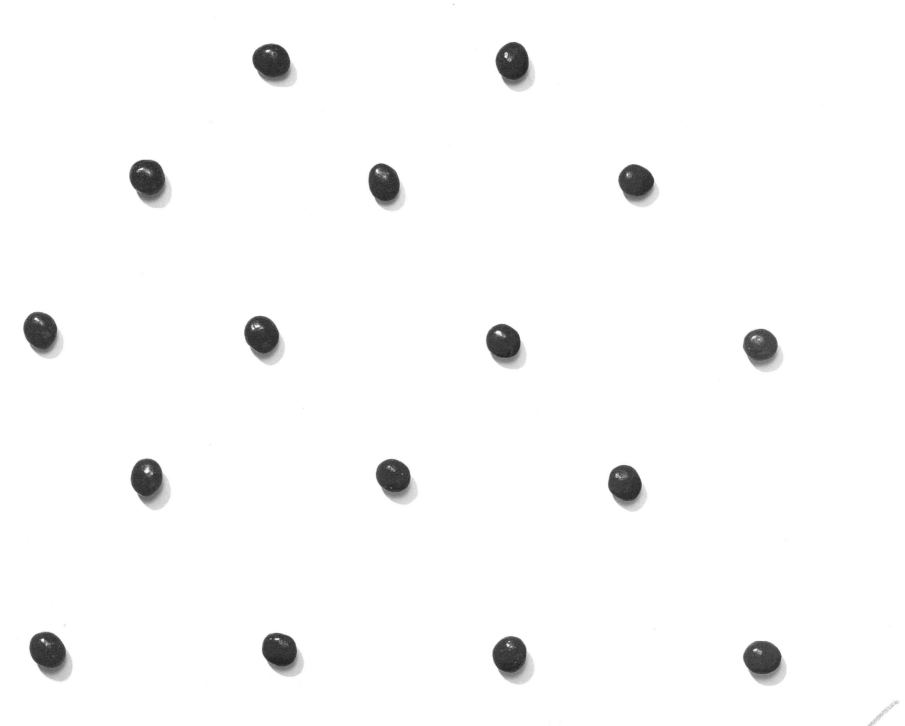

Your grandma makes the best fudge in the world. She cuts it into 20 pieces. You invite your 3 best friends over to share it. But your big sister brings home her 8 best friends to share it, too! If every friend gets 1 piece, how many pieces are left for you and your sister?

It's Halloween, and you have 24 candy corns. Your dad swipes 2 candy corns and sticks them on his teeth like a vampire. He jumps out of the bushes and scares a trick-or-treater, who crashes into you. That trick-or-treater makes you spill 10 candy corns. How many do you have left?

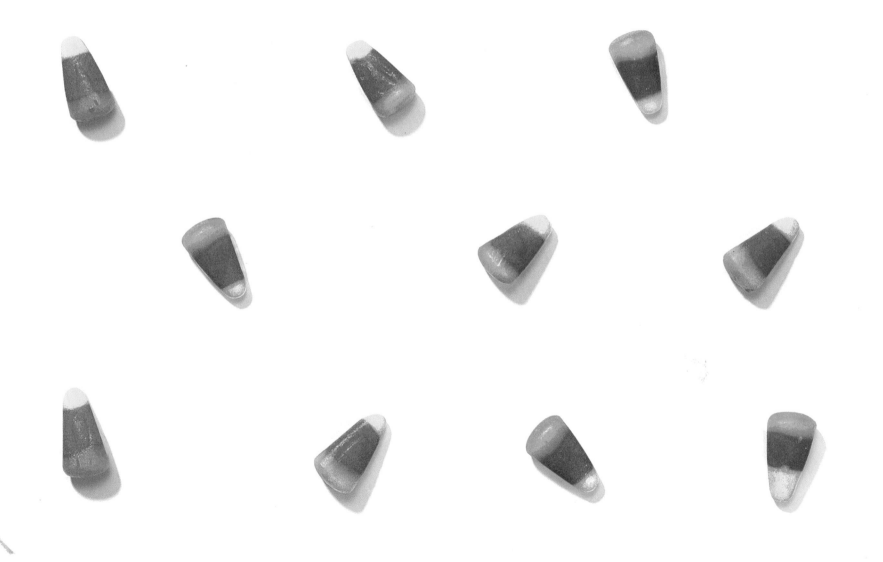

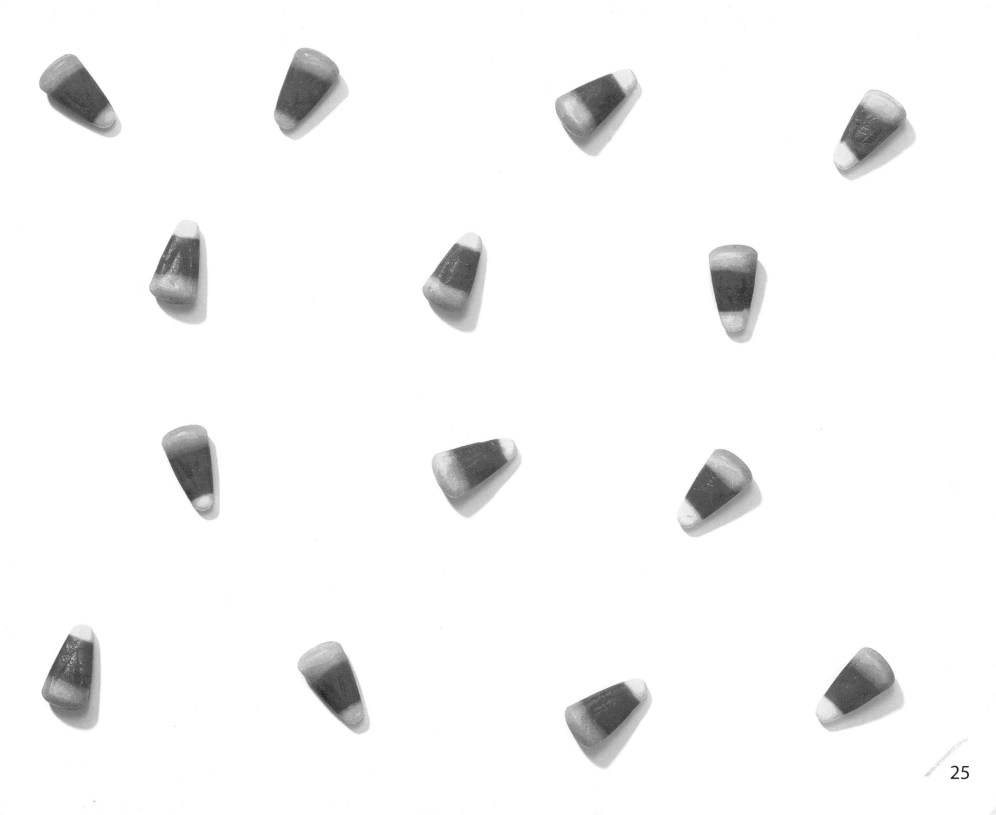

It's the 100th day of school! To celebrate, each student in your grade brings 1 piece of candy to school. Ms. Petunia has 33 students in her class. Mr. Rumpus has 32 students. Ms. Dinkle has 35 students. How many pieces of candy does your entire grade have?

27

Did you like the game? Want to know a secret? It was all math! Look on the next four pages to see how you did. If you were right about how to get the answer but got the wrong answer, don't worry. The most important thing is to figure out how to figure it out! That's math, sweet and simple.

Here's the math!

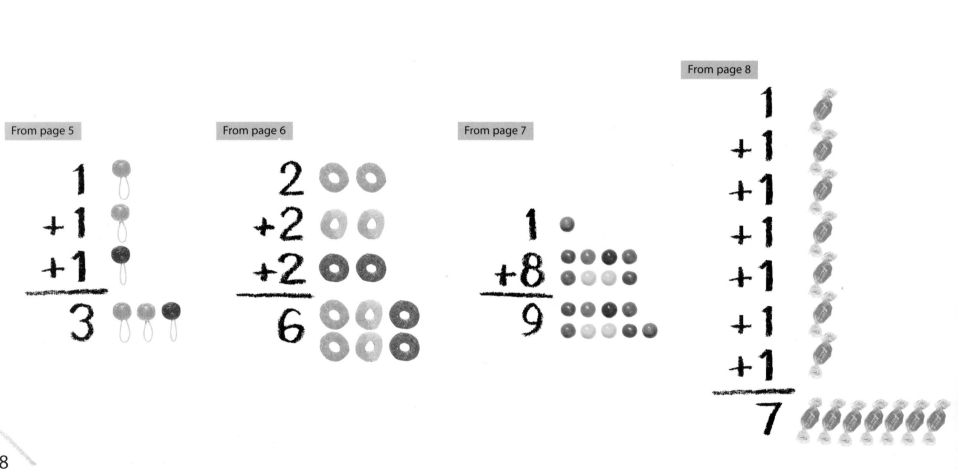

From page 5

$$\begin{array}{r} 1 \\ +1 \\ +1 \\ \hline 3 \end{array}$$

From page 6

$$\begin{array}{r} 2 \\ +2 \\ +2 \\ \hline 6 \end{array}$$

From page 7

$$\begin{array}{r} 1 \\ +8 \\ \hline 9 \end{array}$$

From page 8

$$\begin{array}{r} 1 \\ +1 \\ +1 \\ +1 \\ +1 \\ +1 \\ +1 \\ \hline 7 \end{array}$$

28

From page 9

$$4$$
$$+2$$
$$\overline{6}$$

From page 9

$$4$$
$$-2$$
$$\overline{2}$$

From pages10 & 11

$$10$$
$$-6$$
$$\overline{4}$$

From page 12 & 13

$$30$$
$$-30$$
$$\overline{0}$$

From pages 14 & 15

$$18$$
$$-1$$
$$-1$$
$$\overline{16}$$

29

From pages 16 & 17

28
+1
+1
――
30

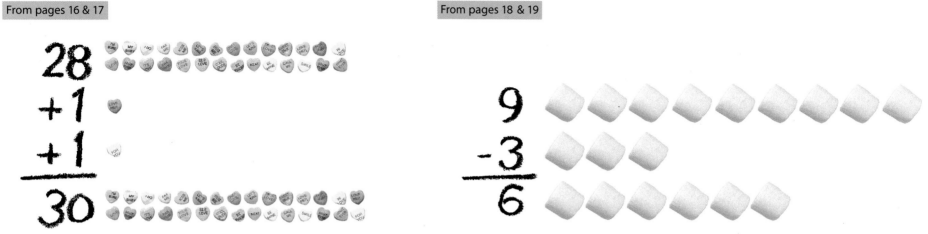

From pages 18 & 19

9
-3
――
6

From pages 20 & 21

6
+20
――
26

From pages 20 & 21

26
-10
――
16

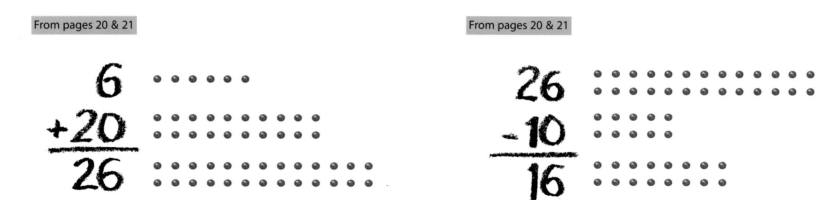

From pages 22 & 23

20
−3
−8
____
9

From pages 24 & 25

24
−2
−10
____
12

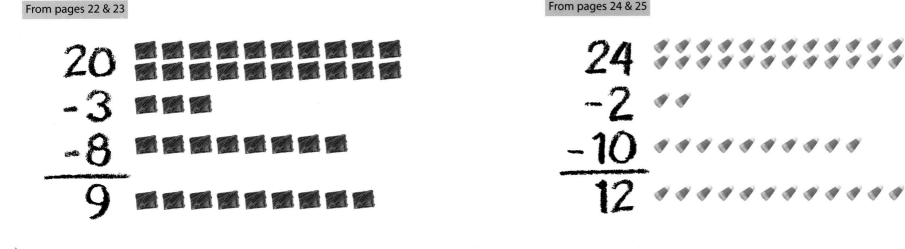

From pages 26 & 27

33
+32
+35
____
100

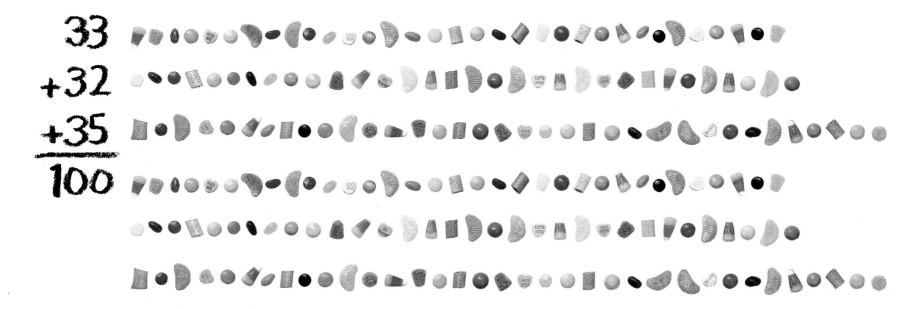

Candy-Counting Activities
for Grown-Ups to Do with Kids

• • •

Here are some suggestions for more counting fun in your child's daily life:

● Have your child count how many pieces of popcorn he or she eats during the first Coming Attraction at the movie theater. During the next trailer, let your child count how many pieces you eat. How many did you eat together?

● Bake cookies and let your child count them. When it is time to taste the cookies, ask your child to keep track of how many are eaten, and then ask him or her to figure out how many are left.

● Fill a small jar with jellybeans. Have your child count the jellybeans. Then make a chart. At the top write the quantity of jellybeans in the full jar. Each day, log the number of jellybeans left in the jar. Help your child subtract the number left from the starting number to determine how many were eaten each day.

● Don't limit yourself to candy! Counting fun is all around. Try counting:

  • *the number of legs in your family.* Be sure to include pets' legs! Ask your child to add all the legs together. How many are there?
  • *wheels.* See how many wheels your child can spot in three minutes. Don't forget to add up wheels on bicycles, toy trucks, and in-line skates!
  • *collections.* For example, if you collect teapots and your child collects stuffed animals, have him or her count each collection and add the totals of both collections together.